Written and Illustrated by
Cathleen Reid
AKA Gramma Doodle

This book is dedicated to Mikayla Schwartz, Kyle Schwartz, Ava Lynn Schwartz and Brylee Ann Schwartz.

The Magic of Spring Two is all about the baby birds as they learn about flying.

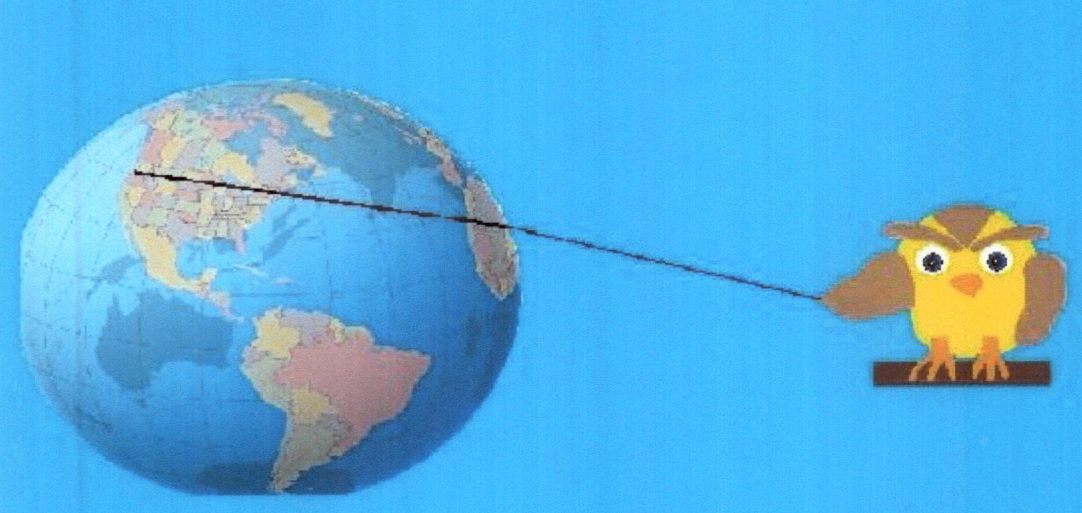

Once upon a time on a small spot on the Earth, in the little town of Kelso Washington there was a farm.

Mother Mikayla and father Kyle were
so happy that the baby birds were
hatched.

Mother bird looked at father bird and said what do you think we should name the babies?

Let's name this baby AvaLynn said
father bird.

Ok said mother bird and lets name
this one Brylee. Ok said father bird.
And so it was AvaLynn and Brylee.

Avalynn and Brylee grew
and grew until they could
get out of the nest.

One day father bird brought home a worm for the babies to eat.

AvaLynn said I can't eat that cute wiggly worm. Brylee put out her wing, I will take it she said.

Brylee took the wiggly worm and said we will keep him for a pet.

Brylee said do you think we will be able to learn to fly soon?

I am afraid to fly said Brylee. It will be fun said AvaLynn. I think you just put out your wings and then you fly.

Willy played on the branch while
the baby birds talked about flying.

Willy said watch me do a trick, he hung upside down on the branch.

Father and mother bird heard the
babies and came to help.
A rabbit heard the birds and came to
join them.

Everyone cheered you made it said
father bird.

AvaLynn flapped her wings but she was not strong enough yet to make it back up to the nest.

Raccoon, owl and rabbit asked if they could help.

Cow, horse and sheep followed father bird back to the tree.

Squirrel, chipmunk, duck, pig, owl and rabbit followed raccoon back to the tree.

All the animals got
on each others back,
and baby bird climbed
back up to the top of
the tree.

Father bird told raccoon and rabbit that it was time to teach the baby birds to fly.

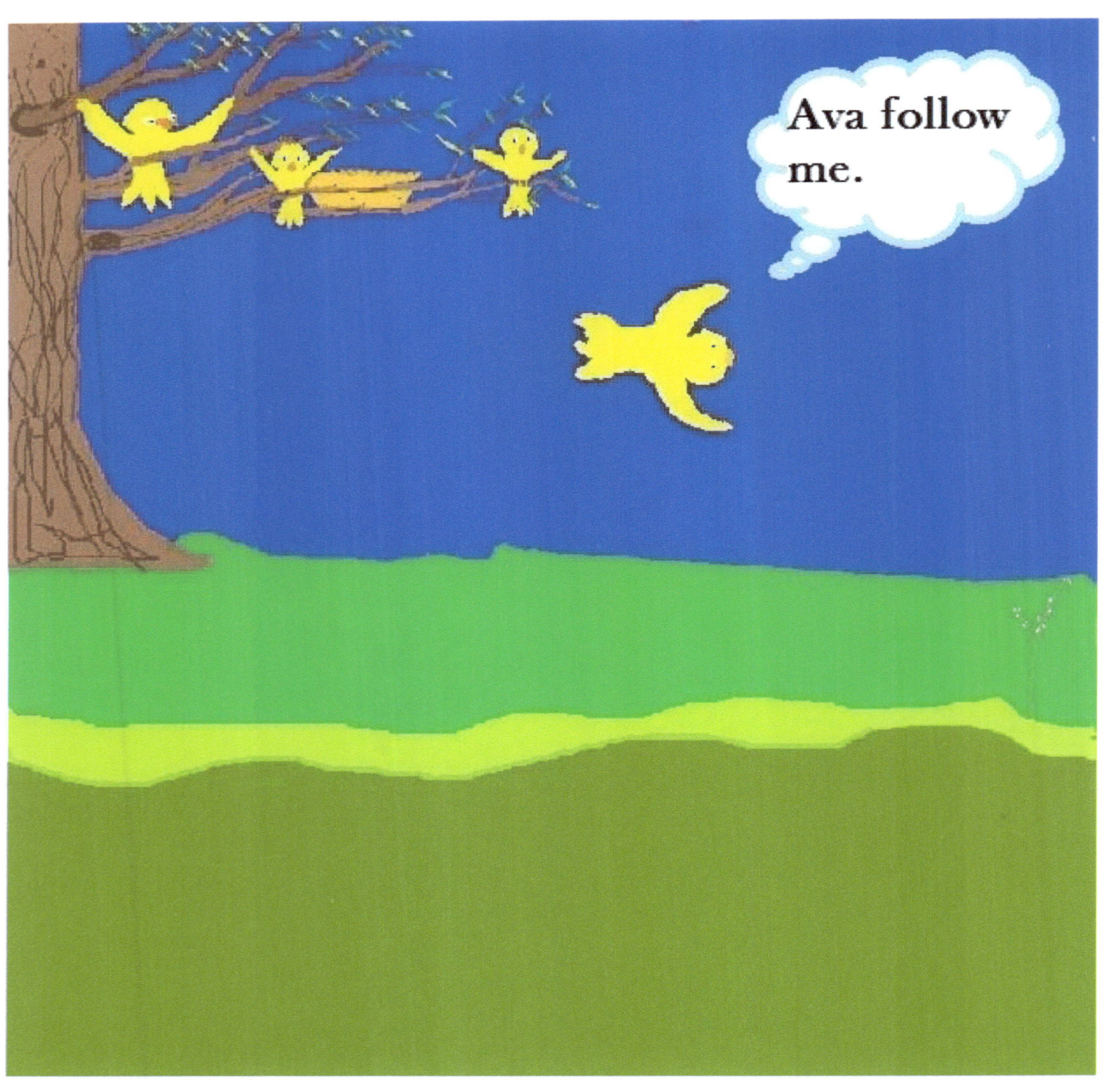